This Journal Belongs to

Donna K. Maltese

MY

Bible Study

JOURNAL

JOY

180 Bible Readings to Strengthen Your Faith

BARBOUR BOOKS
An Imprint of Barbour Publishing, Inc.

Joy is more than a feeling; it is a deep peace, blended together with a solid hope that God has not left us. Joy is a delight in knowing there will be a better day.

KAROL LADD, *THE POWER OF A POSITIVE WOMAN*

Welcome to *My Bible Study Journal: Joy*, a place where you can commune with God, His Word, and the Holy Spirit as you seek and embark on your pathway to joy. This is your entrance into a quiet time of prayer, reading, and reflection, a way of discovering what God is speaking into your life and what He is revealing to you and you alone.

This book contains six topical 30-day Bible reading plans (one page per day) in the following areas to help you find, focus on, and follow God's path to joy:

Each of the 180 days contains that day's specific aspect of joy, a scripture reading, and two or more journaling prompts.

Before beginning each day's Bible passage, *pray* for the Holy Spirit's illumination. Make it your intention to *listen* to what God is saying. Then and only then, *absorb* the Bible passage for that day.

Afterward, before looking at any commentary or considering that day's journaling prompts, *mark* the verse or passage that specifically speaks to your heart in this place and time—whether or not you understand why. Then go on to the journaling prompts. Carefully read each one, then *reflect* on and *respond* to the prompt that most speaks to you—or to the verse you have already marked—and see what more God may reveal. The point is to follow where God is leading as you journey to joy. At the end of your journaling time, pray for God to embellish in your own heart, soul, and life the truths He has imparted. Ask for His strength and courage to go where He's leading.

Within these pages you have the opportunity to take hold of your God, life, voice, thoughts, purpose, dreams, spirit, study journal, and pen. Trust that you will find the path, the clue, the word to be followed as your joy unfolds.

*May the God of your hope so fill you with all joy and peace
in believing [through the experience of your faith] that
by the power of the Holy Spirit you may abound
and be overflowing (bubbling over) with hope.*
ROMANS 15:13 AMPC

30 DAYS OF BIBLE READINGS FOR

JOY
Defined

*Be not grieved and depressed, for the joy
of the Lord is your strength and stronghold.*
NEHEMIAH 8:10 AMPC

There are two kinds of happiness. The first depends on what is happening around us, what our circumstances are. The second is based on a calm assurance that *no matter what* is happening, we're trusting Jesus, confident of the Holy Spirit's help and presence, and convinced God will work all things out for our good. It's about rising above the earthly fray and man's machinations, finding our way to the unspeakable happiness that's found only in God—true, heavenly, peace-inducing joy. It's knowing that, no matter how dark things seem, God's light is illuminating a path of safety and contentment.

In the thirty readings that follow, you'll explore what joy is. As you enter your time in God's Word, disregard any Bible commentary. This will allow God to speak to you one-on-one, heart-to-heart, page-by-page. Begin with a prayer to God, something like, "Here I am, Lord, a lover of Your Word. Speak. I'm listening." Then read the scripture, *expecting* God to reveal Himself to you. Meditate on what you've read. Underline the word, phrase, or sentence that pulls at your heart. Then quietly reflect on and honestly respond to the journaling prompt of your choice. Afterward, thank God for the moments you've shared and ask Him to help you apply what you've learned.

JOY DEFINED — DAY 1

Joy Is Your Strength—Part 1

Read Nehemiah 8:1-10

God's once-captive people wept as His Word was read and explained to them. What emotions sweep over you when you read scripture?

....

....

....

....

....

....

....

The people's leader—not wanting their spirits to flag, leaving them too weak to overcome difficulties—reminded the people where their strength lies: in the joy of their Lord. Where does your strength lie?

....

....

....

....

....

....

....

JOY DEFINED — DAY 2

Joy Is Your Strength—Part 2

—————————— *Read Nehemiah 8:1–10* ——————————

Some Bible translations read, "The joy of the LORD is your strong-hold" (Nehemiah 8:10 HCSB), a place of shelter. How does knowing that you can run to God and be assured protection give you joy?

....

....

....

....

....

....

How does rejoicing because you have protection from an all-powerful God increase your strength and confidence?

....

....

....

....

....

....

....

Joy Is Your Strength—Part 3

—————— Read Nehemiah 8:10–12 ——————

Hearing God's Word made His people realize how far they'd mis-stepped in His eyes. Yet only when encouraged to rejoice instead of mourn could they switch their focus from their failings and weakness to His forgiveness and strength. What might you need to do to change your own focus from self-condemnation to joy-filled celebration?

....

....

....

....

....

....

In what way has a better understanding of God's Word led you to rejoicing?

....

....

....

....

....

....

JOY DEFINED — DAY 4

Joy Is What God Prompts You to Do

——————— *Read Nehemiah 12:27–43* ———————

God's people celebrated the dedication of Jerusalem's newly built wall, rejoicing because "God had given the people cause for great joy" (Nehemiah 12:43 NLT). In what specific ways does God give *you* cause for great joy?

....

....

....

....

....

....

When God's people rejoiced, it "could be heard far away" (Nehemiah 12:43 NLT). When was the last time you rejoiced regardless of your volume or appearance?

....

....

....

....

....

....

....

Joy Is Commanded by God—Part 1

——————— *Read Deuteronomy 26* ———————

How often do you acknowledge that all you've received has come from God's hands? In what ways may you have helped or hindered His efforts?

....
....
....
....

Whom do you credit for all the ways you've been rescued from dire situations?

....
....
....
....

In what ways could you and your household follow God's command to rejoice for all the blessings He's given you?

....
....
....
....

Joy Is Commanded by God—Part 2

———— *Read Deuteronomy 28* ————

Moses told God's children that if they didn't serve God with a joyful heart because of His abundant provisions, they'd end up serving their enemy in lack (Deuteronomy 28:47–48). How might this knowledge affect your own attitude when you serve God?

....
....
....
....
....
....
....

What do these verses tell you about the God you serve?

....
....
....
....
....
....
....

Joy Is a Response by Believers for God's Forgiveness

—————— *Read Psalm 32:1–6, 11* ——————

In what ways do you suffer when you keep silent, not wanting to tell God about a misstep you made?

....

....

....

....

What kind of relief do you experience when you finally fess up to God?

....

....

....

....

What does your joy meter read when you realize that God not only forgives your sins but also clears you of all guilt?

....

....

....

....

Joy Is a Response by Believers for God's Love—Part 1

—————— *Read Psalm 32:7–11* ——————

God promises to "guide you along the best pathway for your life" and to "advise you and watch over you" (Psalm 32:8 NLT). How has He done this in the past? in the present?

....

....

....

....

....

....

In what ways or during what times might God consider you "like a senseless horse or mule that needs a bit and bridle to keep it under control" (Psalm 32:9 NLT)?

....

....

....

....

....

....

....

Joy Is a Response by Believers for God's Love—Part 2

—————————— *Read Psalm 32:7–11* ——————————

The psalmist said, "Unfailing love surrounds those who trust the LORD" (Psalm 32:10 NLT). Imagine God and His love enveloping you. How might that lift your heart?

....
....
....
....
....
....

Those who are obedient to and honest with God are to rejoice in Him and be glad. What might you need to share with God today so that you too can experience joy?

....
....
....
....
....
....
....

Joy Is a Response by Believers for God's Defending Them

—————— *Read Psalm 64* ——————

Words are very powerful. On a scale of one to ten, with one being the lowest and ten the highest, how sensitive are you to what others say to and about you?

....

....

....

....

....

....

In what ways might you react to people who suddenly attack you with their words? How might that change if you took refuge in God?

....

....

....

....

....

....

....

Joy Is a Response by Believers for God's Delivering Them

—— *Read Psalm 63* ——

When you're in trouble, whose strength and help do you rely on? Why?

....

....

....

....

The psalmist sought God, thinking about Him day and night, recognizing Him as his helper. In what ways has God been your helper?

....

....

....

....

Imagine God protecting you as a mother bird protects her chicks. How might this lead you to not just peace but also a time of rejoicing in the shadow of His wings?

....

....

....

....

Joy Is a Response by Believers to God's Word

— *Read Psalm 119:1–16* —

When have you found yourself wandering off the path God laid out before you in His Word?

....

....

....

Have you ever considered "pre-praying"—asking God to keep you from wandering from His commands *before* you veer off in the wrong direction?

....

....

....

Which verses in God's Word have you treasured so that you wouldn't sin against Him?

....

....

....

Why might you find joy in following God's instructions?

....

....

Joy Is a Response by Believers to God's Help

———————— *Read Isaiah 41:8–16* ————————

As God's chosen servant, you needn't fear. He has promised to help, strengthen, and uphold you. Imagine the Creator of the universe holding you by your right hand. What feelings bubble up deep within?

....

....

....

....

....

....

....

How might your life change if you took God's promise to heart, memorizing and believing His words, "Don't be afraid. I am here to help you" (Isaiah 41:13 NLT)?

....

....

....

....

....

....

Joy Is Something to Pass Along

—————————————— *Read Job 29:11–16* ——————————————

Have you ever helped someone no one else would help? How did that person respond?

....

....

....

What feelings are generated within you when you're helping someone else?

....

....

....

Has your help ever made someone else's heart rejoice? If so, what were the particulars?

....

....

....

What would it feel like to be "eyes to the blind and feet to the lame" (Job 29:15 HCSB)?

....

....

Joy Is a Fruit of the Spirit

—————— *Read Galatians 5:13–23* ——————

In Galatians 5:22, Paul listed love as the first fruit of the Spirit. Why might that attribute take precedence over all the others?

....

....

....

....

The second fruit is joy. Why do you think joy is second only to love?

....

....

....

Why might the spiritual fruit of peace follow next?

....

....

....

Which of these nine godlike attributes is strongest in you? Why?

....

....

....

Joy Is Nature's Response to God

—————— *Read Psalm 65* ——————

When God visits the earth, He drenches its ground and streams with water, thus reviving it, making it more productive. In what ways does God visit you? How do those encounters revive you? How might they make you more productive for Him?

....
....
....
....
....
....
....

In what ways do you think nature—hills, meadows, valleys, mountains—reveals joyfulness? In what ways do you reveal joyfulness?

....
....
....
....
....
....

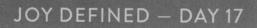

Joy Is to Be Shouted About

—————— *Read Psalm 66* ——————

God wants you to "shout joyfully" (Psalm 66:1 HCSB), to tell others all the amazing things He has done that have made you rejoice in Him. When was the last time you did so?

....

....

....

....

....

List at least three specific things God has done or provided that brought you joy.

....

....

....

....

With whom will you share that list today?

....

....

....

....

Joy Is to Be Shared with God—Part 1

—————— *Read Matthew 25:14–30* ——————

What opportunities, abilities, or resources has God given you? Have you used them to serve God? If so, how? If not, why not?

....

....

....

....

....

....

....

If you *have* used your "talents" (things entrusted to you) to serve God, in what ways did doing so increase His initial investment in you? If you have *not*, how did that choice detract from God's work?

....

....

....

....

....

....

....

Joy Is to Be Shared with God—Part 2

—————— Read Matthew 25:14–30 ——————

How might people's perception of God lead them into taking the safest course of action (burying talents) instead of stepping out of their comfort zone (using talents)?

....
....
....
....
....
....

When you use your talents to serve God, He invites you to share in His joy. What does that look like and feel like to you?

....
....
....
....
....
....
....

Joy Is What God Does When You Seek Him

——————— Read Zephaniah 3:11–17 ———————

Why would God remove the proud from the humble?

....

....

....

....

....

In what areas of your life might you be more satisfied than seeking?
How would your life change if you became humble in *every* area?

....

....

....

....

....

How would it feel to live each day with an awareness that almighty
God—who delights in you—is in your midst?

....

....

....

....

Joy Is What God Does When You Trust Him

———————— *Read Zephaniah 3:11–17* ————————

God wants you to trust Him so much that you'll never again fear evil. What does your current fear meter read? Why?

....

....

....

....

What might it look like to be quieted by God's love? What might it be like to rejoice in Him as He rejoices over you?

....

....

....

....

What might God's "joyful songs" (Zephaniah 3:17 NLT) sound like? Why not sing one back to Him?

....

....

....

....

Joy Is What Comes with the Morning

Read Psalm 30:1–5

God's anger lasts a moment but His favor a lifetime. How does this encourage you in your walk with Him?

....

....

....

....

How would your life change if you lived it certain that sorrow is temporary and joy long-lasting?

....

....

....

....

In what ways do you find God's mercies new every morning (Lamentations 3:22–23)? How might knowledge of morning mercies bring you to a place of joy?

....

....

....

....

Joy Is What God Converts from Sorrow

——————— *Read John 16:20–22* ———————

When, if ever, have you found yourself weeping while others rejoiced? What were the particulars?

....

....

....

....

When have you looked back on a painful event that seemed unbearable at the time but you now realize was the best thing that ever could have happened?

....

....

....

....

How might the certainty that your weeping will be turned into laughter help you face the future?

....

....

....

....

JOY DEFINED — DAY 24

Joy Is Something That Can Never Be Taken from You

———— *Read John 16:20–22* ————

When, during a time of anguish, have you remembered a treasured promise of God, one that immediately lifted your spirits? What was that promise?

....

....

....

....

What verses might you store in your heart now to help you in the future?

....

....

....

....

How does it feel knowing that Jesus, God the Father, and the Spirit have given you a joy that can never be taken away from you?

....

....

....

Joy Is What God Clothes You In

———————— *Read Psalm 30:6–12* ————————

When has God turned your mourning into dancing?

....

....

....

....

....

When has God taken away your black mourning clothes and dressed you up in joy?

....

....

....

....

How might knowing that God has the power to lift you from the darkness and lead you into His light give you peace in the present and help you prepare for the future?

....

....

....

....

JOY DEFINED — DAY 26

Joy Is What Happens When God Turns Things Around

———— Read Esther 8 ————

God has a way of turning things upside down. When have you witnessed someone's evil intentions backfire?

....

....

....

....

How does this part of Esther's story give your heart not just joy but also hope?

....

....

....

....

What is currently happening in your life that you'd like God to turn around?

....

....

....

....

Joy Is Celebrated

Read Esther 9:20-32

God Himself is not mentioned in the book of Esther, although His handiwork is obvious. He was behind it all when the Jews' "sorrow was turned into rejoicing and their mourning into a holiday" (Esther 9:22 HCSB). Do you celebrate God when He turns things around in your life? If so, what does that look like? If not, why not?

....

....

....

....

....

....

....

How might celebrating God's work in your life improve your life?

....

....

....

....

....

....

Joy Is Experienced When Taking Refuge in God

—— *Read Psalm 5* ——

What does taking refuge in God look like to you? What do you experience there?

....

....

....

....

In what ways does God spread His protection over you? When do you recognize Him defending you the most?

....

....

....

....

What does it feel like knowing that God not only makes His way straight before you but also surrounds you with His shield of love?

....

....

....

....

Joy Is Experienced When in God's Presence

—————— *Read Psalm 16* ——————

Have you ever seen "the sorrows of those who run after another god. . .multiply" (Psalm 16:4 ESV)?

....

....

....

....

In what ways do you "set the LORD always before" you (Psalm 16:8 ESV)? How does doing so keep you from being shaken up? How does this prompt your spirit to rejoice?

....

....

....

....

How does God's presence give you "fullness of joy" (Psalm 16:11 ESV)?

....

....

....

....

Joy Is Always Available and Accessible

—————————— *Read 2 Corinthians 8:1–5* ——————————

What troubles have tested you in the past? What troubles are testing you today?

....

....

....

How can you continue to be filled with joy, during good and not-so-good times?

....

....

....

In what ways, if any, do you find joy to be abundant *and* always available and accessible?

....

....

....

List three things that give you joy. Why do they give you joy?

....

....

....

30 DAYS OF BIBLE READINGS FOR

Discovered

Up to this time you have not asked a [single] thing in My Name [as presenting all that I Am]; but now ask and keep on asking and you will receive, so that your joy (gladness, delight) may be full and complete.
JOHN 16:24 AMPC

God wants your joy to be full and complete—just as His is. So, He gives you several ways and places to discover joy. Some may surprise you. Others may be avenues to joy that you've neglected or forgotten.

As you embark on this second of six 30-day Bible reading plans, you'll journey through finding joy in gratitude, in God's presence, in nature, within your own sorrow, and so much more!

Just as in the first section, as you enter your time in God's Word, leave Bible commentary or notes out of your conversation with God. Doing so will allow Him to speak to you one-on-one, heart-to-heart, page-by-page. Begin with a prayer to God, something like, "Here I am, Lord, a lover of Your Word. Speak. I'm listening." Then read the scripture, *expecting* God to reveal Himself to you. Meditate on what you've read. Underline the word, phrase, or sentence that pulls at your heart. Then quietly reflect on and honestly respond to the journaling prompt of your choice. Afterward, thank God for the moments you've shared and ask Him to help you apply what you've learned.

In Gratitude

———————— *Read Psalm 95* ————————

How do you express your joy to people? How is that different from expressing your joy to God? What "joyful noise" might you make in expressing your pleasure to and for God?

....

....

....

....

How has God been a Rock for you? What song might you write in praise of that Rock?

....

....

....

....

List the things you're grateful for yesterday and today. How does doing so change your perspective of yesterday? today?

....

....

....

....

In God's Presence

—————————— *Read Exodus 33* ——————————

Author George MacDonald wrote, "Few delights can equal the mere presence of one whom we trust utterly." In what ways do you utterly trust God?

....

....

....

....

....

....

Moses said to God, "If it is true that you look favorably on me, let me know your ways so I may understand you more fully and continue to enjoy your favor" (Exodus 33:13 NLT). How might increasing your knowledge of God increase your enjoyment of Him?

....

....

....

....

....

....

In Your Faith

———————— *Read Romans 5:1-11* ————————

Because of your faith in Jesus, you've "been made right in God's sight" (Romans 5:1 NLT). What kind of peace does this lead to? How might that peace then lead you into joy?

....

....

....

....

When, if ever, have you rejoiced while in trouble? How might that rejoicing have changed your perspective—and the outcome of your situation?

....

....

....

....

Because of Jesus, you're in a new relationship with God called friendship. What does that look like to you?

....

....

....

....

In Helping Others

——————— *Read Acts 20:18–35* ———————

In what ways have others worked to support you in the past? In what ways have you worked to support yourself? others?

....

....

....

....

....

When and how do you help the weak or less fortunate?

....

....

....

....

Jesus said, "It is more blessed (makes one happier and more to be envied) to give than to receive" (Acts 20:35 AMPC). When have you found that to be true? Whom can you help today?

....

....

....

....

In Nature

—————————— Read Psalm 96:11–12 ——————————

Way before scientists discovered the benefits of forest bathing, God knew trees would increase our joy and happiness. That's why He inspired the psalmist to write, "Let the trees of the forest sing for joy" (Psalm 96:12 NLT). How do you immerse yourself in nature?

....

....

....

....

In what ways have you found being in nature instrumental to your joy?

....

....

....

....

What song of joy could you share with God's creation?

....

....

....

....

In Forgetting

——————— *Read Isaiah 43:18–19* ———————

God does many things "for your sake" (Isaiah 43:14 AMPC), including helping you forget things that have already passed. What one thing do you have trouble forgetting?

....

....

....

....

What new thing is God doing in your life? In what ways is it a new path through the wilderness for you?

....

....

....

....

How might God's creating something new prompt you to "sing a new song of praise to him. . .with joy" (Psalm 33:3 NLT)?

....

....

....

....

In Great Expectations

—————————— *Read 1 Peter 1:1–7* ——————————

Because God raised Jesus from the dead, you can expect that He will one day raise you. How high does that great expectation register on your joy meter?

....

....

....

....

In what ways do you feel that God "is protecting you by his power" (1 Peter 1:5 NLT)?

....

....

....

....

How does knowing the joy of heaven that lies ahead of you help you get through today's troubles?

....

....

....

....

In Loving and Believing in Jesus

—————————— Read 1 Peter 1:8-9 ——————————

Why do you, without ever having seen Him, love Jesus? What makes you believe in Him?

....

....

....

....

What is it about Jesus that makes you trust Him? How does that trust prompt you to "rejoice with a glorious, inexpressible joy" (1 Peter 1:8 NLT)? What reward does that trust in Jesus bring you (1 Peter 1:9 NLT)?

....

....

....

....

What things or people do you *entrust* to Jesus?

....

....

....

....

In Your Sorrow

————— *Read 2 Corinthians 6:1–10* —————

How do knowledge, patience, and kindness help you through difficulties?

....

....

....

....

How does the influence of the Holy Spirit, the Word, love, and God's power help you overcome obstacles?

....

....

....

....

God's ministers were described as being "sorrowful, yet always rejoicing; as poor, yet making many rich; as having nothing, yet possessing everything" (2 Corinthians 6:10 ESV). When and in what ways has this been true for you?

....

....

....

....

In Relationships with Others

———————— *Read 2 John* ————————

What emotions do you experience when you see the children of another believer walking in God's truth (2 John 4)?

....

....

....

....

....

Why is meeting a friend, relative, or lover face-to-face more powerful than a text, email, letter, or phone call? How does such a one-on-one connection make your joy complete (2 John 12)?

....

....

....

....

Whom do you feel called to reach out to today?

....

....

....

....

In Realizing the Need for Jesus

—————— *Read Luke 15:3–10* ——————

Jesus said there's an amazing amount of joy in heaven when one lost person discovers they need Jesus. What do you think that heavenly celebration looks like?

....

....

....

....

How have you celebrated when you found something you'd lost?

....

....

....

....

What joy did you experience when you found Jesus? How wonderful was it when you, through Him, found your way to God? What, if any, joys have been greater?

....

....

....

....

In Asking

—————— Read John 16:20–24 ——————

Jesus said His Father would "grant you whatever you ask" in His name (John 16:23 AMPC). How often do you end your prayers with "in Jesus' name, amen"? How might doing so become more automatic than meaningful?

....

....

....

....

....

....

....

Jesus said you're to "ask and keep on asking and you will receive, so that your joy. . .may be full" (John 16:24 AMPC). In what ways are you a persistent prayer?

....

....

....

....

....

....

In Life Itself

———— *Read Ecclesiastes 9:7-10* ————

How often do you take joy in the simple things in life—such as eating and drinking or chasing a firefly?

....

....

....

....

....

When was the last time you got dressed up? When was the last time you went out with a friend or the love of your life?

....

....

....

....

How would your life change if you started taking joy in all things—big and little?

....

....

....

....

In Hope

—————— *Read Proverbs 10:28* ——————

When an obedient child of God expectantly waits, she does so joy-fully. She knows her waiting time will end in joy because God gives her good things. Not so for the ungodly, whose eager hopes and expectations will come to nothing. What are you waiting for right now? What are your expectations?

....

....

....

....

....

....

....

Are you finding joy within the waiting? Why or why not?

....

....

....

....

....

....

In a Good Night's Sleep

Read Psalm 4

How have you been sleeping lately?

....

....

....

....

How might saying, "The LORD will answer when I call to him" (Psalm 4:3 NLT) and remembering the joys He's given you (Psalm 4:7) help you sleep better?

....

....

....

....

In what ways might adding, "In peace I will lie down and sleep, for you alone, O LORD, will keep me safe" (Psalm 4:8 NLT) to your prayer increase your quality of sleep?

....

....

....

....

In God's Comfort

—————— Read Psalm 94 ——————

How do you handle negative thoughts that come into your head?

....
....
....

What do you do when doubts fill your mind?

....
....
....

The psalmist wrote, "In the multitude of my [anxious] thoughts within me, Your comforts cheer and delight my soul!" (Psalm 94:19 AMPC). How does the God of comfort cheer you?

....
....
....

When have you taken comfort in the fact that God is your High Tower, your Rock of refuge (Psalm 94:22 AMPC)?

....
....
....

In the God of Hope

———— *Read Romans 15:1–13* ————

In what ways is God "the God of your hope" (Romans 15:13 AMPC) or "the source of hope" (Romans 15:13 NLT)?

....

....

....

....

....

Paul prayed that God would fill believers completely with joy and peace because they "trust in him" (Romans 15:13 NLT). Why do you think hope, joy, peace, and trust are so inextricably linked?

....

....

....

....

How much joy and peace are you experiencing in your life?

....

....

....

....

In God Being in Your Midst

———————— *Read Isaiah 12* ————————

How does God comfort you?

....

....

....

In what ways is God not just your strength but also your song (the appropriate object of your praise)? When was the last time you sent God a thank-you "note" through song?

....

....

....

How does God being your strength and song give you courage?

....

....

....

For what will you praise God today? How does that praise increase your joy?

....

....

....

In God's Love, Mercy, and Faithfulness

—————— *Read Lamentations 3:1–26* ——————

Has there ever been a time when you have "forgotten what happiness is" or "become depressed" (Lamentations 3:17, 20 HCSB)? If so, what did you do to turn things around, to regain your hope (Lamentations 3:21)?

....

....

....

....

What new mercy did you discover this morning?

....

....

....

....

In what ways does impatience affect your level of joy and contentment?

....

....

....

....

In the Love of Others

Read Philemon 1–7

Who do you know that exudes love for fellow believers? How does that person demonstrate that love?

....

....

....

....

Why might seeing someone's love for others give *you* joy and comfort? bring others to the faith?

....

....

....

....

How and why do acts of kindness refresh the hearts of others? What kindness can you perform today? How will that draw you closer to God?

....

....

....

....

In Restoration

—— *Read Psalm 51* ——

What misstep do you need to confess to God today?

....

....

....

How might a sin against others be seen as a sin against God alone?

....

....

....

In what ways does admitting your sins to God cleanse you? restore your joy? renew your spirit?

....

....

....

What does it mean to offer God a "broken spirit" and a "humbled heart" (Psalm 51:17 HCSB)? What will you offer God today?

....

....

....

In Giving an Apt Reply

———————— *Read Proverbs 15* ————————

How often do body parts appear in your Bible's translation of Proverbs 15? Which are related to what you say—to God, yourself, and others?

....

....

....

....

How many times do you leave a conversation and only later come up with the words you feel you *should've* said?

....

....

....

....

How might being a believer help you say the right thing at the right time more often?

....

....

....

....

In the Kingdom of God

— Read Romans 14 —

In what ways might disagreements about communion bread—its quality, contents, form, etc.—become a stumbling block for a weak believer?

....

....

....

....

What three qualities describe the kingdom of God in Romans 14:17?

....

....

....

....

How hard is it for you to keep your convictions about food and drink to yourself? What would God rather have you focus on, aim for, and attempt to do?

....

....

....

....

In Affliction

———— *Read 2 Corinthians 7:2–16* ————

In what ways have you been encouraged and found joy in your walk with God, even amid affliction?

....

....

....

....

....

When you're "troubled in every way: conflicts on the outside, fears inside" (2 Corinthians 7:5 HCSB), from whom or what do you receive comfort? Who or what gets the credit for that comfort?

....

....

....

....

In what ways do you find joy to be contagious?

....

....

....

....

In Smiles

——————— *Read Proverbs 15:30* ———————

Why do you think God made both smiles and frowns contagious? Which are you doing right now?

....

....

....

In a world full of bad news, where do you look for good news? In what ways does good news refresh you?

....

....

....

What can you do today, besides smiling, to bring joy into another person's life?

....

....

How will spreading joy in the lives of others bring joy into your own life?

....

....

....

In Walking God's Way

—————— *Read Psalm 97* ——————

In what ways has God been shining His light on you and your plans? How has He been planting seeds of joy in your heart?

....

....

....

....

God provides "joy for the upright in heart [the irrepressible joy which comes from consciousness of His favor and protection]" (Psalm 97:11 AMPC). When have you experienced "irrepressible joy"?

....

....

....

....

What might you do to maintain a constant awareness of God's favor and protection?

....

....

....

....

In Giving Back to God

Read 2 Corinthians 9

In what ways do you make a contribution to God's family? Do you do so cheerfully, deciding in your heart how much to give? Or do you do so "reluctantly or in response to pressure" (2 Corinthians 9:7 NLT)?

....

....

....

....

....

How do you feel after you share what you have with others?

....

....

....

....

In what ways does giving to others bring you joy?

....

....

....

....

In Encouraging Others

—————— *Read Philippians 1:1–11* ——————

How would you feel if you heard that someone was praying for you *and* making requests for you with joy?

....

....

....

....

....

What changes for you when you get encouragement from others? In what ways do you and can you encourage fellow believers?

....

....

....

....

Whom can you encourage today? How might doing so increase your own joy?

....

....

....

....

In Wisdom

—— *Read Proverbs 3:13–26* ——

What are you doing to increase your understanding and knowledge of God?

....

....

....

....

Why might wisdom be more valuable to you than silver, gold, and rubies?

....

....

....

....

In what ways do you think of wisdom as "a tree of life to those who embrace her" (Proverbs 3:18 NLT)? Do you embrace wisdom? If so, are you finding your joy increased as you "hold her tightly" (Proverbs 3:18 NLT)?

....

....

....

....

In Your Name Written in Heaven

—————— *Read Luke 10:1–20* ——————

Your name is written somewhere here on earth. But how does it feel knowing your name is actually written down in heaven?

....

....

....

....

....

How often and in what ways might you feel like an alien on earth?

....

....

....

....

....

When do you feel like you're more of a citizen registered in heaven than one on earth?

....

....

....

....

30 DAYS OF BIBLE READINGS FOR

JOY
in Jesus

Rejoice greatly, Daughter Zion! Shout in triumph, Daughter Jerusalem!
Look, your King is coming to you; He is righteous and victorious,
humble and riding on a donkey, on a colt, the foal of a donkey.
ZECHARIAH 9:9 HCSB

Jesus is linked to joy. After all, joy permeated His predicted coming, actual arrival, short-lived life, foreseen death, amazing resurrection, and awe-inspiring ascension. Even now, we cannot help but celebrate and rejoice in the joy we find in Jesus!

As you embark on this third of six 30-day Bible reading plans, you'll find where our joy begins and never ends—in Jesus. You'll see how joy in Jesus can be contagious, how it can go from being delayed by doubt to buoyed by understanding!

Just as in the previous sections, as you enter your time in God's Word, leave Bible commentary or notes out of your conversation with God. Doing so will allow God to speak to you one-on-one, heart-to-heart, page-by-page. Begin with a prayer to God, something like, "Here I am, Lord, a lover of Your Word. Speak. I'm listening." Then read the scripture, *expecting* God to reveal Himself to you. Meditate on what you've read. Underline the word, phrase, or sentence that pulls at your heart. Then quietly reflect on and honestly respond to the journaling prompt of your choice. Afterward, thank God for the moments you've shared and ask Him to help you apply what you've learned.

In a Great Light

Read Isaiah 8:19–9:7; Matthew 4:12–17

The prophet Isaiah linked distress with darkness (Isaiah 8:22) and joy with a shining light (Isaiah 9:2–3). In what ways did Jesus, "a child. . . born to us, a son. . .given to us" (Isaiah 9:6 NLT), first bring light into your life?

....

....

....

....

....

In what ways does He lighten or enlighten your life today?

....

....

....

....

Which of Jesus' titles in Isaiah 9:6 speak to you most? Why?

....

....

....

....

Because of His Rescue and Ministry

Read Isaiah 35:1-6; Matthew 11:2-6

Isaiah predicted Jesus' coming to rescue God's people. How does your faith rescue you?

....

....

....

....

....

In what ways might you be waiting for or expecting someone else— other than God or Jesus—to come and save you?

....

....

....

....

How has God opened your eyes, cleared your ears, and made you shout for joy?

....

....

....

....

By His Proclamation

—————— *Read Isaiah 61:1; Luke 4:16–21* ——————

After reading from Isaiah 61:1–2, Jesus proclaimed He was the expected Messiah, the One "anointed. . .to bring Good News to the poor" (Luke 4:18 NLT), to heal hearts and free captives. When has Jesus comforted you or been on hand to bind up your broken heart?

....

....

....

....

....

In what ways have Jesus and His Good News set you free?

....

....

....

....

What might still be holding you in bondage?

....

....

....

....

Entered in Triumph

— *Read Zechariah 9:9; Matthew 21:8-10; Luke 19:28-40* —

Although a king, Jesus didn't arrive in Jerusalem with costly robes, a fine horse, or a regal chariot. He came in humbly, dressed casually, on a donkey. How might those realizations change your perspective of Jesus?

....

....

....

....

....

....

Even though Jesus' entry was humble, people still rejoiced in His presence. When was the last time you joyfully celebrated Jesus' presence in your life?

....

....

....

....

....

....

....

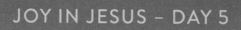

Deviated by Disloyalty

—————— *Read Zechariah 11:12–13; Matthew 27:1–10* ——————

When Judas the betrayer realized Jesus the innocent had been condemned to death, as predicted by Zechariah, "he was filled with remorse" (Matthew 27:3 NLT). When has a guilty conscience—over a big or little misstep, misjudgment, or misdeed—stolen your joy? To whom, if anyone, including God, did you confess your mistake?

....

....

....

....

....

....

....

What actions, if any, did you take to set things right?

....

....

....

....

....

....

....

Delayed by Doubt

———— *Read Luke 1:5–24, 67–80* ————

Gabriel told Zechariah that he and his aging wife, Elizabeth, would have the son they'd been praying for and "great joy and gladness. . . at his birth" (Luke 1:14 NLT). But because Zechariah couldn't believe the angel, the elderly priest was mute until John was born. When has *your* joy been delayed by doubt?

....

....

....

....

....

....

....

What might you have lost because of it?

....

....

....

....

....

....

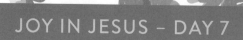

Buoyed by Understanding

—————— *Read Luke 1:26–38* ——————

Gabriel greeted Mary by saying: "Rejoice, favored woman! The Lord is with you" (Luke 1:28 HCSB). Not knowing what he meant left Mary very troubled. So Gabriel then told her, "Do not be afraid" (Luke 1:30 HCSB). In what ways has a lack of knowledge or understanding left you troubled?

....

....

....

....

....

....

How does God's phrase *do not fear* or the words *God is with you* feed or expand your joy?

....

....

....

....

....

....

Can Be Contagious

— *Read Luke 1:39–46* —

When has the obvious joy of another person filled *you* with joy?

....

....

....

When, if ever, has your joy *and* the indwelling of the Holy Spirit led you to proclaim a blessing on another person?

....

....

....

Elizabeth was very humble. How might her blessing have been received if she'd given it from a place of smugness?

....

....

....

Whom can you bless and share your joy with today?

....

....

....

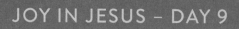

Because You Believe

——————— *Read Luke 1:37, 45–56* ———————

Gabriel had told Mary about Elizabeth's pregnancy then said, "Nothing will be impossible with God" (Luke 1:37 HCSB). How do these words increase your faith in God?

....

....

....

....

Elizabeth's blessing of Mary—"You're blessed because you believed God would do what He said" (paraphrase)—paved the way for Mary to burst out in a song of rejoicing. What do Elizabeth's words do for you?

....

....

....

....

How might singing a song proclaiming God's power strengthen you?

....

....

....

Amid Unusual Happenings

—————— *Read Luke 1:57–80* ——————

When the elderly Elizabeth gave birth to a son, her neighbors and relatives gave all the credit to God and rejoiced with her (Luke 1:58). When might you forget to give God credit for your joy?

....

....

....

....

....

....

....

John the Baptist's birth and life were anything but usual and caused people to fear and wonder (Luke 1:65–66). How might fear, prompted by unusual happenings, affect your joy?

....

....

....

....

....

....

From Good News

—————— *Read Luke 2:1–14* ——————

How does it feel knowing that, no matter what your status or standing in the world, God can and will use you for big things?

....

....

....

....

....

In what ways does getting good news—and being the first one to hear it—increase your joy?

....

....

....

....

How has Jesus become "good news of great joy" (Luke 2:10 ESV) for you? How did you recognize Him when He entered your life?

....

....

....

....

Following the Light

———————— *Read Matthew 2:1–12* ————————

The magi are said to have been pagans. How does the fact that God used heathens in His grand plan increase your faith in Him and His ways?

....

....

....

....

Why might the powerful sometimes be "deeply disturbed" (Matthew 2:3 NLT) when they get word of Jesus?

....

....

....

....

When you followed God's light and found Jesus, how did you respond? In what ways did you then find yourself more attuned to God and His wisdom?

....

....

....

....

Rising Up

——————— *Read Matthew 3:13-17* ———————

Jesus insisted that John baptize Him, saying, "It should be done, for we must carry out all that God requires" (Matthew 3:15 NLT). Afterward, as Jesus rose up out of the water, a voice from heaven said, "This is my dearly loved Son, who brings me great joy" (Matthew 3:17 NLT). In what ways does Jesus bring you great joy?

....

....

....

....

....

....

....

How determined are you to do as God requires, thus bringing *Him* great joy?

....

....

....

....

....

....

JOY IN JESUS – DAY 14

And the Kingdom

—————— *Read Matthew 13:44–46* ——————

In this passage, Jesus told two parables about what the kingdom of heaven is like—and how those who find it are filled with joy. What joy has finding Jesus and the kingdom given you?

....

....

....

....

....

In what ways is God's kingdom precious to you?

....

....

....

....

What would you sell to secure God's kingdom? What would you give (or have you given) to obtain it?

....

....

....

....

As the Prodigal—Part 1

——————— *Read Luke 15:11–31* ———————

When, if ever, have you felt too unworthy to be called God's daughter or a follower of Jesus? How did you get to that place—or are you still there?

....

....

....

....

What happened (or may need to happen) to bring you back to your senses, like the Prodigal Son?

....

....

....

....

Have you ever mentally rehearsed a speech to God in which you ask Him for forgiveness? What incongruity might you find in that?

....

....

....

....

As the Prodigal—Part 2

Read Luke 15:11–31

Have you ever had God interrupt your prayer of contrition with an overwhelming "I forgive you" moment or feeling?

....

....

....

....

....

What emotions pour over you when you envision God as a father filled with love and compassion, running to welcome you into his arms—and then sharing the best he has with you?

....

....

....

....

In what ways might you celebrate your "return" to God's arms?

....

....

....

....

Who Seeks the Lost—Part 1
Read Luke 19:1-10

Have you ever been (or are you now) hard-pressed to get even a glimpse of Jesus? What stood (or stands) in your way? What did (or can) you do to get a better look?

....

....

....

....

....

When have you felt Jesus looking at you? speaking to you? inviting Himself in for a visit?

....

....

....

....

In what ways might you open yourself up to Jesus at His request?

....

....

....

....

Who Seeks the Lost—Part 2

— *Read Luke 19:1-10* —

Have others ever made you feel you weren't worthy to be part of their community of believers?

....

....

....

In what ways, if any, do *you* feel you might have fallen short in the eyes of Jesus?

....

....

....

When have you done something just for Jesus? What was that something?

....

....

....

How joyful are you that Jesus came to seek and save you?

....

....

....

Through Childlike Faith

——— *Read Luke 10:17–24* ———

In what ways does God reveal Himself to you?

....
....
....
....
....

Each day you have the opportunity to learn a little more about God, either through His Word or His work. How can you savor those aha moments? celebrate them? record them?

....
....
....
....

God has chosen to reveal Himself and His ways to *you*. In what ways have you, in turn, revealed yourself to *Him*?

....
....
....
....

As You Remain in Him

——— *Read John 15:1–17* ———

What do you do to remain in Jesus as He remains in you (John 15:4)? What can you do to ensure Jesus' words remain in you? What is your reward?

....

....

....

....

....

....

....

Jesus said that when you obey Him, you will be filled with His joy *and* "your joy will overflow" (John 15:11 NLT)! How might this assurance help you follow Jesus' command during difficult times?

....

....

....

....

....

....

Because of His Prayer for You

———— Read John 17 ————

How does knowing you are in the keeping power of both God and Jesus give you a sense of peace?

....
....
....
....
....

You have the Bible, a record of what Jesus taught His followers. What is it about Jesus' Word that fills you with joy?

....
....
....
....

How does it feel knowing Jesus' prayer was meant for all His followers (John 17:20)—including you?

....
....
....
....

Comes to Women at the Tomb

— *Read Matthew 28:1–10* —

In what ways do you take comfort in the fact that both angels and Jesus seek to calm our fears (Matthew 28:5, 10) before all else?

....

....

....

....

....

The angel told the women that Jesus had risen "just as he said would happen" (Matthew 28:6 NLT). What clue does this give you about the value of God's words?

....

....

....

....

When have you experienced awe mingled with joy?

....

....

....

....

Behind Closed Doors

— *Read John 20:19–23* —

In what ways have you received both comfort and courage from Jesus?

....
....
....

When has Jesus found a way to reach you, even when you've closed Him off intentionally or unintentionally?

....
....
....

How does knowing that Jesus Himself was wounded—yet remained whole—while here on earth give you courage, peace, and joy?

....
....

What can you do to continually remind yourself that Jesus is with you, God is watching you, and the Holy Spirit lives within you?

....
....
....

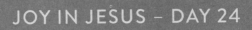

When You Believe without Seeing

———— *Read John 20:24-29* ————

When have you not believed something until you saw proof with your own two eyes?

....

....

....

....

....

....

....

Jesus said, "Blessed and happy and to be envied are those who have never seen Me and yet have believed" (John 20:29 AMPC). What joy does it give you knowing that Jesus blessed you over two thousand years ago—*and* that you can still experience the effects of that blessing today?

....

....

....

....

....

....

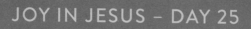

With Opened Minds

—— *Read Luke 24:36–49* ——

Even after Jesus showed His followers His hands and feet, "they still disbelieved for joy and were marveling" (Luke 24:41 ESV). When has Jesus shown you something, yet you still had trouble believing? What did it take to convince you?

....
....
....
....
....
....
....

In what ways does Jesus open your mind so that you can understand the scriptures? What do you do to give Him access to your heart and mind?

....
....
....
....
....
....

Ascending

———————— *Read Luke 24:50–53* ————————

Luke began his book with a fearful, unbelieving muted priest (Luke 1:12–20) and ended it with faith-filled disciples cheering and watching as Jesus, while blessing them, was taken up to heaven. In what ways, if any, does this resemble your own journey of faith?

....

....

....

....

....

....

As Jesus was lifted up to heaven, He continued to bless His joy-filled followers. Right now, in this moment, how is Jesus continually blessing you?

....

....

....

....

....

....

....

By Diving Right In

—————— *Read John 21:1-14* ——————

When have you been so disheartened in your faith walk that you went back to your old ways? What was the result?

....

....

....

....

....

In what ways do you recognize Jesus working in your life today, pointing you toward abundance?

....

....

....

....

How does your joy in and love for Jesus make you dive right in to get close to Him—no matter what the water temperature?

....

....

....

....

In His Name

—————— *Read Acts 3:1-10* ——————

As Peter and John neared the temple, a lame man, begging for alms at the gate, "paid attention to them, expecting that he was going to get something from them" (Acts 3:5 AMPC). When have you been expecting one thing, only to find God has something much bigger and better in mind?

....

....

....

....

What does this account tell you about Jesus' name?

....

....

....

....

How have unexpected blessings from God led you to joyful praise?

....

....

....

....

While Running the Race

—————— Read Hebrews 11:1–12:2 ——————

Which hero in the hall of faith (Hebrews 11) do you most identify with? Why?

....

....

....

What weight might you need to cast aside so it won't trip you up in your walk with God?

....

....

....

What might be distracting you, keeping you from fixing your eyes and mind on Jesus?

....

....

....

How does focusing on "the joy awaiting" (Hebrews 12:2 NLT) help you through difficult times?

....

....

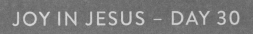

Inspired by the Spirit

—————— *Read 1 Thessalonians 1:1–7; 2:19–20* ——————

In what ways has your faith led you to both joy and suffering? How might your joy amid suffering have made you an example for others?

....

....

....

....

....

What faithful follower would you choose (or have you chosen) to imitate in some way? Why?

....

....

....

....

How does the Holy Spirit inspire joy in you? How do you inspire joy in the lives of others?

....

....

....

....

30 DAYS OF BIBLE READINGS FOR

JOY
Makers and Breakers

He hushes the storm to a calm and to a gentle whisper, so that the waves of the sea are still. Then the men are glad because of the calm, and He brings them to their desired haven.
PSALM 107:29–30 AMPC

Some things contribute to the creation of joy in your life, such as God's Word, His presence, and unexpected aid. Other things—such as pride, worry, or anguish—can bend, if not break, your joy.

As you embark on this fourth of six 30-day Bible reading plans, you'll discover things that might trip you up along the way (distractors and detractors) and things that might smooth your path (builders and boosters) to experiencing joy—here and beyond!

Just as in the previous sections, as you enter your time in God's Word, leave Bible commentary or notes out of your conversation with God. Doing so will allow God to speak to you one-on-one, heart-to-heart, page-by-page. Begin with a prayer to God, something like, "Here I am, Lord, a lover of Your Word. Speak. I'm listening." Then read the scripture, *expecting* God to reveal Himself to you. Meditate on what you've read. Underline the word, phrase, or sentence that pulls at your heart. Then quietly reflect on and honestly respond to the journaling prompt of your choice. Afterward, thank God for the moments you've shared and ask Him to help you apply what you've learned.

God's Presence and Power

———————— *Read Acts 11:19-30* ————————

When the Jerusalem church heard that God's presence and power were with believers in Antioch, they sent Barnabas (meaning "Son of Encouragement" [Acts 4:36 AMPC]) there. He, overjoyed at what was unfolding, encouraged the people to stay faithful. When does your joy lead you to encourage others?

....

....

....

....

....

....

When you do encourage others, how does it affect you, your joy, and your walk with God?

....

....

....

....

....

....

Faithful Recognition

———— *Read Acts 14:1–20* ————

When people look straight at you, do they see your faith shining through? How has someone's recognition of your faith transformed your life?

....

....

....

....

What worthless things do you need to turn from so that you can turn to God? What steps might you take to do so?

....

....

....

....

What, besides a joy-filled heart, has God given you as evidence of Him and His goodness?

....

....

....

....

A Common Cause

———————— Read 1 Chronicles 12 ————————

Mighty men joined up with David "until he had a great army" (1 Chronicles 12:22 NLT). The rest of Israel was of a single mind to support him as well, all of which created "joy in Israel" (1 Chronicles 12:40 AMPC). When have you experienced joy when involved in a common cause? How was your joy expressed?

....

....

....

....

....

....

How much more precious might such an experience have been knowing God was behind it?

....

....

....

....

....

....

Realization of Blessings

Read Deuteronomy 16

God commanded His people to hold certain celebrations—such as the Feasts of Unleavened Bread, Weeks, and Booths—so the Israelites would remember what God had done for them. What has God done for you this week? this month? How will you celebrate?

....
....
....
....
....
....
....

God *orders* His children to rejoice and be joyful before Him (Deuteronomy 16:11, 14–15 ESV). How might that move rejoicing up on your list of to-dos?

....
....
....
....
....
....

God's Presence

———— *Read 1 Chronicles 16:1–36* ————

When you endeavor to seek Yahweh, do you do so gladly, with a heart that's rejoicing?

....

....

....

....

What would your joy meter read if you made it a priority to "seek the LORD and his strength; seek his presence continually" (1 Chronicles 16:11 ESV)?

....

....

....

....

David sang, "Honor and majesty surround him; strength and joy fill his dwelling" (1 Chronicles 16:27 NLT). In what ways do you find that to be true for you?

....

....

....

....

Jehoshaphat–Part 1: Humble

—————— *Read 2 Chronicles 20:1-30* ——————

After hearing of an imminent invasion of his kingdom, the first thing Jehoshaphat of Judah did was seek God. What's the first thing you do when hearing bad news?

....

....

....

....

....

....

Jehoshaphat was humble enough to pray, "We do not know what to do, but our eyes are on you" (2 Chronicles 20:12 ESV). How might that statement inevitably have become a joy maker?

....

....

....

....

....

....

....

Jehoshaphat—Part 2: Standing Still

——————— *Read 2 Chronicles 20:1–30* ———————

In response to Jehoshaphat's prayer, God spoke through Jahaziel, saying, "You will not even need to fight. Take your positions; then stand still and watch the LORD's victory" (2 Chronicles 20:17 NLT). When, if ever, have you stood still, leaving room for God to move for you?

....

....

....

....

....

....

....

How does knowing God is with you keep you from becoming fearful, discouraged, and joyless?

....

....

....

....

....

....

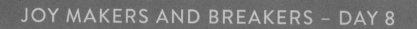

Jehoshaphat—Part 3: Standing Firm

—— *Read 2 Chronicles 20:1–30* ——

On the day of battle, Jehoshaphat told his people, "Believe in the LORD your God, and you will be able to stand firm" (2 Chronicles 20:20 NLT). How might your faith and commitment to God's way pave your way to joy?

....

....

....

....

....

....

....

After the enemy armies annihilated each other, only the spoils were left to be picked up. What spoils have you received from God's battling for you?

....

....

....

....

....

....

Acting from the Heart

—————— *Read 2 Chronicles 29* ——————

King Hezekiah had it in his heart to bring his people back to God. When was the last time your heart prompted you to do something for God? What action did you take?

....

....

....

....

....

....

Hezekiah started his temple and the restoration of his people from the inside out. In the end, all rejoiced because "God had prepared the people" (2 Chronicles 29:36 HCSB). In what ways might God be preparing you for joy?

....

....

....

....

....

....

Unexpected Aid from Enemies

———————— *Read Ezra 6* ————————

The temple completed, the Jews "kept the Feast of Unleavened Bread seven days with joy, for the LORD had made them joyful and had turned the heart of the king of Assyria to them" (Ezra 6:22 ESV). When has God transformed the heart of your former enemy into that of a new friend?

....

....

....

....

....

....

....

How did that person's change of heart strengthen your hands or lead you to joy?

....

....

....

....

....

....

A Good Laugh

——————— *Read Job 8* ———————

When has God "fill[ed] your mouth with laughter and your lips with shouts of joy" (Job 8:21 NLT)? What were the circumstances?

....

....

....

....

Think back to a time when you were suffering some sort of hardship. In what ways could you now consider those days somewhat joy filled?

....

....

....

....

What can you do today to fill someone else's mouth with laughter and her lips with joy?

....

....

....

....

God's Word

—————— *Read Psalm 19* ——————

In what ways does God's creation speak to you? What have the heavens, the stars, and the sun said to you lately? How have they given you joy?

....

....

....

....

....

....

The psalmist said God's Word can revive the soul, make the simple wise, make the heart rejoice, and enlighten one's eyes. Think about your favorite verses from God's Word. Which ones fit all the aspects the psalmist wrote about?

....

....

....

....

....

....

Witness Writings

—————— *Read 1 John 1:1–5; 2 John 12* ——————

The apostle John was there with Christ, seeing, touching, hearing Him. What weight do those facts give to the words John wrote and spoke?

....

....

....

....

What do you think John meant when he described Jesus as "the Word of life"?

....

....

....

....

In what ways does sharing what we know about Jesus become a source of amazing joy—for the sharer and listener? Whom can you witness to today?

....

....

....

....

Children Walking in Truth

—————— *Read 2 John 4; 3 John 1–4* ——————

Consider all the things that give you joy. Then list your joy makers from greatest to least.

....

....

....

....

....

....

....

Did the joy you get when you see friends, family, and fellow believers walking in the truth (3 John 4) make it onto your list? Why or why not? What does that reveal to you?

....

....

....

....

....

....

....

Forgiveness

Read Romans 4:1–17

Imagine a list of all your misdeeds being read over a public-address system. What emotions come up for you?

....

....

....

....

How does it feel not just to be forgiven for your missteps but also to have them "put out of sight" (Romans 4:7 NLT), your record wiped clean by God?

....

....

....

....

One way to spread the joy of forgiveness you've received from God is to forgive others. Whom do you need to forgive today?

....

....

....

....

Focusing on Former Things

—————— *Read Ezra 3* ——————

When formerly exiled Jews laid the foundation of the new temple in Jerusalem, the priests began praising God. But elders who remembered the majesty of the former temple began weeping. Yet the ones who had never seen the temple rejoiced! How can you keep former things from dampening your or another's joy?

....

....

....

....

....

....

....

If misery steals your joy, what steps can you take to recover it?

....

....

....

....

....

....

Pride

———————————— *Read Esther 5* ————————————

Haman, a scheming egotist determined to annihilate the Jews, was "joyful and glad of heart" (Esther 5:9 ESV) because of Queen Esther's dinner invitation. But the fact that Mordecai neither rose in respect nor trembled in fear when Haman walked by filled him with rage. When, if ever, has pride sucked out your newfound joy?

....

....

....

....

....

....

....

What *good* thing did you (unlike Haman) do to recover your joy—or was that experience of joy gone forever?

....

....

....

....

....

....

Discipline

──────── *Read Hebrews 12:1–13* ────────

How well do you respond to discipline from those who raised you? How do you react when Father *God* disciplines you?

....

....

....

....

....

When have you made light of God's reprimand? When, if ever, have you lost courage or given up because of it?

....

....

....

....

Hebrews 12:11 (AMPC) says that "no discipline brings joy" yet later it does bear fruit. When have you found this to be true?

....

....

....

....

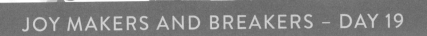

Dissing Soul Watchers

Read Hebrews 13:1–17

Who was the first person to teach you God's Word and exemplify Christ? What good came of following that person's example of faith? To whom might you now be an example of Christ?

....

....

....

....

....

....

Consider your current spiritual leaders whose work is to watch over your soul. In what ways do you "give them reason to do this with joy and not with sorrow" (Hebrews 13:17 NLT)?

....

....

....

....

....

....

Worry—Part 1

———————— *Read Philippians 4:4-9* ————————

Paul knew very well that, if allowed, worry could block the path to continual joy. Thus, he told believers not to worry or be anxious. Instead, they were to pray. When trouble darkens your door, what's your first reaction—panic or prayer? What is the result of panic? of prayer?

....

....

....

....

....

....

....

When was the last time you thanked God for all He's done? How did you feel afterward?

....

....

....

....

....

....

Worry—Part 2

—————— *Read Philippians 4:4-9* ——————

To follow the command to rejoice, you're advised not to worry about anything but to pray about everything. To thank God for all He's done. How will those things lead you to "experience God's peace" (Philippians 4:7 NLT)?

....

....

....

....

How would you describe what God's peace is like?

....

....

....

....

In what ways does this peace beyond understanding guard your heart and mind?

....

....

....

....

On the Edge with Anguish—Part 1

Read 1 Samuel 1:1–2:11

When have your own personal challenges, mingled with the comments and actions of a bully, caused you great mental, emotional, and spiritual anguish? What did you do to cope?

....
....
....
....
....
....
....

When was the last time you were so distraught that you fell to your knees and poured out your heart to God? What resulted from that knee-bending encounter?

....
....
....
....
....
....

On the Edge with Anguish—Part 2

Read 1 Samuel 1:1–2:11

When has someone's encouragement and blessing sparked an increase in your faith and brightened up your outlook?

....

....

....

....

When has God answered a desperate prayer and given you your heart's desire? In what ways did you express your joy and give Him thanks?

....

....

....

....

When have you realized your blessing was actually part of God's grand plan—for you *and* others?

....

....

....

....

Clearing Pathways

——— *Read Genesis 39* ———

Joseph was thrown into a pit by his brothers, sold, enslaved, and imprisoned. *Yet* he continued to find his solace in God, who "was with Joseph, so he succeeded in everything he did" (Genesis 39:2 NLT). Where do your thoughts lead you when everything seems to be going against you? Where do you seek solace?

....

....

....

....

....

....

....

What can you do to hang on to God's *yet* and thus clear your pathway to joy?

....

....

....

....

....

....

Forgiveness vs. Unforgiveness

———————— *Read Genesis 50* ————————

Even after all the things his brothers did against him, Joseph forgave them, telling them not to be afraid. For God took their actions and worked them for good. With his words, Joseph "comforted them [imparting cheer, hope, strength]" (Genesis 50:21 AMPC). When has your forgiveness brought relief to you and joy to the one forgiven?

....

....

....

....

....

....

....

To whom do you need to extend forgiveness today? From whom might you need to ask forgiveness?

....

....

....

....

....

....

Hushed Storms

———— *Read Psalm 107:21–30* ————

When have you felt as if you were on a rocking boat in a storm? Did your courage melt?

....

....

....

....

How certain were you that God would hush your storm to a calm (Psalm 107:29)?

....

....

....

....

Once you were settled in God's stillness, how long before you joyfully realized He'd also brought you to your "desired haven" (Psalm 107:30 AMPC)? What does that reveal about your God?

....

....

....

....

Divine Direction

Read Proverbs 29:18

When have you been unable to see where God was directing you? How did that affect your decision-making and planning? What effect did it have in your walk with God?

....

....

....

....

....

....

When did you realize that your vision, directions, and instruction could be found in God's truths? How did following those truths lead you not just to a plan but also to joy?

....

....

....

....

....

....

....

The Company You Keep

—————————— *Read Proverbs 29:3, 6* ——————————

In what ways does your love of God's wisdom bring joy to yourself and others?

....

....

....

....

....

....

....

When has the company you've kept led you down the wrong road, further away from God and joy? When has a companion been ensnared in a trap that led to destruction, yet you escaped that same trap, shouting for joy? What enabled you to obtain your freedom?

....

....

....

....

....

....

Hearts of the Matter

— *Read Proverbs 12:4, 20, 25* —

Proverbs 12:4 says a wife's character affects her husband's life. Reflect on your own marriage or that of another. How does this prove to be true?

....

....

....

....

....

How does the state of someone's heart affect that person's actions? How does one person's actions affect the state of another's heart?

....

....

....

....

What words can you say today to lift yourself and others?

....

....

....

....

Wisdom

—— *Read Proverbs 8* ——

Wisdom was watching when God created the earth and skies. What does that tell you about the extent and value of her knowledge?

....

....

....

....

Where do you go for wisdom? Why is the person who listens to Wisdom (as personified in Proverbs) embarking on the path to joy?

....

....

....

....

When it comes down to humankind's earthly wisdom going one way and God's supernatural wisdom going another, which path seems easier?

....

....

....

....

30 DAYS OF BIBLE READINGS FOR

JOY

Cultivating Joy

*[We pray] that you may be invigorated and strengthened with
all power according to the might of His glory, [to exercise]
every kind of endurance and patience (perseverance and
forbearance) with joy, giving thanks to the Father.*

COLOSSIANS 1:11–12 AMPC

Knowing what joy is and how to find it is one thing. But it's a whole other thing to understand how to plant a seed of joy and then grow and develop it. That's what this section will explore.

As you embark on this fifth of six 30-day Bible reading plans, you'll increase and shore up your joy by lifting yourself up by love, following God's will, resting in His presence, and more!

Just as in the previous sections, as you enter your time in God's Word, leave Bible commentary or notes out of your conversation with God. Doing so will allow God to speak to you one-on-one, heart-to-heart, page-by-page. Begin with a prayer to God, something like, "Here I am, Lord, a lover of Your Word. Speak. I'm listening." Then read the scripture, *expecting* God to reveal Himself to you. Meditate on what you've read. Underline the word, phrase, or sentence that pulls at your heart. Then quietly reflect on and honestly respond to the journaling prompt of your choice. Afterward, thank God for the moments you've shared and ask Him to help you apply what you've learned.

Calm Joy

———————— *Read 1 Corinthians 7* ————————

Paul wrote, "Those who use the things of the world should not become attached to them" (1 Corinthians 7:31 NLT). Where *should* believers' attachment be?

....

....

....

....

How would you rank your attachment to the interests listed in 1 Corinthians 7:29–32? How would putting those things last and God first change your daily perspective?

....

....

....

....

What can you do to not diminish your joy but to calm it, to not make it your main aim?

....

....

....

....

Love Laws

———— *Read 1 Corinthians 13* ————

Paul said love "does not rejoice at injustice and unrighteousness, but rejoices when right and truth prevail" (1 Corinthians 13:6 AMPC). Have you ever cheered the downfall of someone you considered nasty? Why do you think the celebration of a ne'er-do-well's ruination goes against God's love law?

....

....

....

....

....

....

Was there ever a time when you found yourself hating a sin but loving the sinner? How might that perspective have helped you—and the other person?

....

....

....

....

....

....

As a Consequence of Your Faith

Read Philippians 1:19–30

The imprisoned, long-suffering apostle named Paul was ready to die and be with Christ. Yet he knew it was better that he remain alive so he could help other believers make progress and find joy in their faith (Philippians 1:25). In what ways have you found joy in your faith?

....

....

....

....

....

....

....

How do you help others grow and find joy in their faith? How might that buoy your own?

....

....

....

....

....

....

Spreading Joy—Part 1

—————————— *Read Philippians 2* ——————————

Paul continued his letter to the fledgling Philippian believers, telling them to live in love and harmony. Their doing so would fulfill his joy. In what ways do your actions grieve or please your spiritual leaders? What might you begin doing to fulfill their joy?

....

....

....

....

....

....

....

The Philippians' progress made Paul rejoice—even though his own future remained uncertain. How does Paul's commitment to joy in others remind you of Jesus?

....

....

....

....

....

....

Spreading Joy—Part 2

—————————— *Read Philippians 2* ——————————

Even though Paul might soon lose his life, he was full of joy. And he wanted his fellow believers "to share that joy. Yes, you should rejoice, and I will share your joy" (Philippians 2:17–18 NLT). When have you been impressed by someone's joy even amid suffering?

....

....

....

....

....

....

....

Were you able to share in that joy? Why or why not?

....

....

....

....

....

....

....

As Commanded

Read Philippians 4:4-9

Paul ordered believers to "always be full of joy in the Lord. I say it again—rejoice!" (Philippians 4:4 NLT). Paul followed that command with a list of things that Christ followers should do. The first is to always be considerate. How might consideration of yourself and others lead to your joy—or God's?

....

....

....

....

....

....

....

Why did Paul want believers to "let everyone see that you are considerate in all you do" (Philippians 4:5 NLT)?

....

....

....

....

....

....

Clarity from Others

———————— *Read Acts 15:1–35* ————————

A dispute had arisen between Jewish and Gentile believers in Christ: to circumcise or not to circumcise. When Gentile followers in Antioch received the letter announcing circumcision would *not* be required, "there was great joy throughout the church" (Acts 15:31 NLT). What troubling questions do you have about your faith?

....

....

....

....

....

....

What happens when you ignore issues that have "troubled you. . . and unsettled your [heart]" (Acts 15:24 HCSB)? What happens when you seek to resolve them?

....

....

....

....

....

....

Allied to Hope—Part 1

———— *Read 2 Corinthians 1:1–11* ————

In 2 Corinthians 1:7 (AMPC), a link between joy and hope is revealed: "Our hope for you [our joyful and confident expectation of good for you] is ever unwavering (assured and unshaken)." What does this amplification of the word *hope* reveal to you?

....

....

....

....

What do you hope for? How might receiving it bring you joy?

....

....

....

....

What do you hope for others? How might their receiving it bring you and them joy?

....

....

....

....

Allied to Hope—Part 2

———————— *Read 2 Corinthians 1:1–11* ————————

Paul and others experienced their fair share of suffering for their faith. Yet because God rescued them every time, they maintained their "hope (our joyful and confident expectation)" that God would continue to deliver them (2 Corinthians 1:10 AMPC). In what ways has God rescued you from danger—past or present?

....

....

....

....

....

....

....

How confident are you that God will rescue you again? How does that future assurance contribute to your present joy?

....

....

....

....

....

....

The Last Word – Again

———— *Read 2 Corinthians 13:11* ————

In his farewell, Paul again instructed believers to rejoice, then added that they should also grow up in faith, be encouraged, be of one mind, and live in peace. In which of these five areas are you excelling? Which need work?

....

....

....

....

....

....

....

If you satisfy these five conditions, Paul said, "the God of love and peace will be with you" (2 Corinthians 13:11 HCSB). When have you found this to be true?

....

....

....

....

....

....

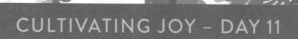

By Meditating on the Word

——————— *Read Psalm 1* ———————

Psalm 1:1 (NLT) lauds "the joys of those who do not follow the advice of the wicked, or stand around with sinners, or join in with mockers." When have you encountered grief and sadness by following society's moral code instead of God's tenets?

....

....

....

....

....

....

....

Do you meditate on God's Word? If so, in what ways do you find delight in that practice? How might it make you prosper?

....

....

....

....

....

....

By Cultivating Confidence—Part 1

—————————— *Read Psalm 27:1–3* ——————————

In what ways has God become your light and salvation as well as your stronghold and refuge?

....

....

....

....

When have you seen your adversaries trip up and lose ground? What did that look like?

....

....

....

....

Are you totally confident that because of God's power and protection, you needn't fear—even if an army surrounds you? How might such confidence lead you to joy? What might that look like to non-believers?

....

....

....

....

By Cultivating Confidence—Part 2

—————— *Read Psalm 27:4-6* ——————

In what ways is God the one thing you seek? What does being a God seeker look like?

....

....

....

....

How does God shelter, hide, and uplift? What sacrifices do you offer Him in return?

....

....

....

....

What songs do you sing to your heavenly Creator, Protector, and Beloved? Do you sing regardless of how it will be received by others? How does such singing for God grow your joy?

....

....

....

....

By Cultivating Confidence—Part 3

—————— *Read Psalm 27:7–12* ——————

How confident are you that God hears your prayers, your requests?

....

....

....

What heart-to-heart conversations have you had with God lately? What prompted them?

....

....

....

When, if ever, have you felt abandoned by others? How confident are you that God will never forsake you? How might you reinforce that confidence?

....

....

....

How does knowing God will always be there *for you* bring you joy?

....

....

....

By Cultivating Confidence—Part 4

——— Read Psalm 27:13-14 ———

Have you ever felt helplessness and hopelessness, as if nothing good was heading your way? What prompted that feeling? What resulted from that joyless combination of attitudes?

....

....

....

....

How would your attitude change if you were truly confident that you would see God's goodness in the land of the living (Psalm 27:13)?

....

....

....

....

Consider memorizing these two verses. Then journal how patience and confidence have restored or increased your hope and joy.

....

....

....

....

With the Shepherd

—————— *Read Psalm 28* ——————

When have you thought God wasn't hearing your prayers? What happened to later convince you otherwise?

....

....

....

....

....

How is God your unyielding strength? In what ways is He your impenetrable shield? How does your confident trust in God help you and prompt your heart to rejoice?

....

....

....

....

When have you felt God shepherding you? How has God carried you?

....

....

....

....

CULTIVATING JOY – DAY 17

By Seeking the Lord

—————— *Read Psalm 34* ——————

In what ways do you seek God? When, where, and how do you do so?

....

....

....

Is praying the first thing you do when fear strikes? Why or why not?

....

....

....

What do you imagine it looks like when the angel of the Lord surrounds you, delivering you from danger and fear?

....

....

....

In what ways does God snuggle up when your heart is broken and your spirit crushed?

....

....

....

Heart Times

—————— *Read Proverbs 14:10, 13* ——————

When has it felt as if no one knows the pain you hold in your heart? When have you realized no one can truly feel the joy you're caught up in?

....

....

....

....

In what ways are you convinced Jesus knows *exactly* how you feel— whether you're joyful or sorrowful? How does that knowledge help you cope with your own state of heart?

....

....

....

....

When have you vacillated between hollow laughter and solid joy?

....

....

....

....

Good Listeners

—————— *Read Proverbs 16:9, 20, 25* ——————

What basic plans do you have for your life? How might God direct your steps as you walk that plan? How does the fact that you decide your plans but God presides over them give you pause or praise?

....

....

....

....

....

....

....

When has listening to God's instruction and trusting Him for all given you joy and success? When has *not* obeying God led you down the wrong road?

....

....

....

....

....

....

No Comparison

——— Read Galatians 6 ———

In Galatians 6:4 (AMPC), Paul urged believers not to compare their work to that of others, for then a believer could have "the personal satisfaction and joy of doing something commendable [in itself alone] without [resorting to] boastful comparison with his neighbor." Have you ever compared your work with that of others? To what did it lead?

....

....

....

....

....

....

....

What joy would you have if you competed against yourself alone?

....

....

....

....

....

....

CULTIVATING JOY – DAY 21

Through Devotions

——————— *Read Acts 2:22–47* ———————

What are some things you devote yourself to? To what do you devote yourself so that you can understand God better? Which "devotions" take priority over others?

....

....

....

What things do you share with fellow believers?

....

....

What does your worship—by yourself and with others—look like?

....

....

....

With what crowds do you gather? Which crowds make you feel better? What joy do you find and express there? What need do they feed?

....

....

....

With Complete Dependence

Read Colossians 1:9-12

What do you believe God's will is for you? How does He impart His wisdom to you?

....

....

....

....

In what ways has God made you stronger than before? What—along with joy—results when you depend completely on God's power? Why might you need those things?

....

....

....

....

How and when do you thank God for all He's done for you? What would a praise party to Him look like?

....

....

....

....

Amid Difficulties

——————— *Read Isaiah 43:1–3* ———————

God, your Lord and Creator, tells you, "Do not be afraid, for I have ransomed you. I have called you by name; you are mine" (Isaiah 43:1 NLT). How does knowing these truths not only give you joy but also ease your mind and heart?

....

....

....

....

....

....

....

When and in what ways did you feel God's presence when you went through rivers of difficulty and fires of oppression?

....

....

....

....

....

....

Lifted by Love

—————— *Read Isaiah 43:3–13* ——————

God said, "Others were given in exchange for you. I traded their lives for yours because you are precious to me" (Isaiah 43:4 NLT). In what ways do these statements make you feel worthy?

....

....

....

....

....

What does it mean that God has made you for His glory?

....

....

....

....

What joy do you take in knowing that God has you in His hands—forever and ever? That no one can snatch you away from Him?

....

....

....

....

On Solid Ground

——— *Read Psalm 40:1–4* ———

When you're patiently waiting for God to hear you, what are your expectations?

....

....

....

In what ways does God lift you out of despair, set your feet on firm ground, and steady your pace?

....

....

....

What new song have you sung to God? In what ways might that have led others to God?

....

....

What joy does trusting God give you? What keeps your confidence in Him instead of in others?

....

....

....

In Doing God's Will

Read Psalm 40:5–10

What wonders has God brought about for you? How long would it take for you to list all He has done in your life?

....

....

....

....

....

In what ways do you find joy in doing God's will? What does it mean to have His instructions written on your heart?

....

....

....

....

Have you shared your journey of faith or God's Good News with anyone? Why or why not?

....

....

....

....

When Surrounded by Trouble

— *Read Psalm 40:11–16* —

Have you ever felt as if all your troubles were surrounding you? In what ways, if any, did those troubles make you lose courage—even if only for a moment? Whom did you cry out to for help? What response did you get?

....

....

....

....

In what ways does searching for God fill you with joy and gladness?

....

....

....

....

What one word would you use to describe God when you're in trouble?

....

....

....

....

By Believing the Unbelievable

—————— *Read Genesis 18:1–21; 21:1–7* ——————

When have you read a promise of God's and laughed at the impossibility of it ever being fulfilled for you? When, if ever, has God called you on it or proven you wrong?

....

....

....

....

When have you felt too far beyond a certain age to find or experience the joy of a certain pleasure? What has God taught you in this regard?

....

....

....

....

In what ways have you realized that *nothing* is too hard for God?

....

....

....

....

By Remembering

—— *Read Psalm 77* ——

When have your troubles been so deep that you couldn't sleep? What did you do in those dark hours? How did you seek comfort?

....

....

....

....

....

....

....

The psalmist thought of "the good old days. . .when [his] nights were filled with joyful songs" (Psalm 77:5–6 NLT). He recollected how well God had led His people. How does realizing that God will *always* be there to lead you bring you to a place of calm, comfort, and joy?

....

....

....

....

....

....

Via Praise and Raise

—————————— *Read Psalm 65* ——————————

When did you last "stand in awe" of God's wonders (Psalm 65:8 NLT)? How does God—His presence and words—inspire you to shout with joy?

....

....

....

....

Author Phillips Brooks wrote, "All the world is an utterance of the Almighty. Its countless beauties, its exquisite adaptations, all speak to you of Him." In what ways do you find this to be wonderfully true?

....

....

....

....

How will you praise God and thus raise yourself today?

....

....

....

....

30 DAYS OF BIBLE READINGS FOR

JOY

Choosing Joy

Though the fig tree does not bud and there is no fruit on the vines, though the olive crop fails. . .yet I will triumph in Yahweh; I will rejoice in the God of my salvation!
HABAKKUK 3:17–18 HCSB

You are now on the last leg of your journaling journey. Here we will explore the decisions you make: to choose joy. . .or not!

As you embark on this final 30-day Bible reading plan, you'll find out the power you have in the decisions you make every day. Professor Randy Pausch said, "You just have to decide whether you are a Tigger or an Eeyore." Which will you be?

Just as in the previous sections, as you enter your time in God's Word, leave Bible commentary or notes out of your conversation with God. Doing so will allow God to speak to you one-on-one, heart-to-heart, page-by-page. Begin with a prayer to God, something like, "Here I am, Lord, a lover of Your Word. Speak. I'm listening." Then read the scripture, *expecting* God to reveal Himself to you. Meditate on what you've read. Underline the word, phrase, or sentence that pulls at your heart. Then quietly reflect on and honestly respond to the journaling prompt of your choice. Afterward, thank God for the moments you've shared and ask Him to help you apply what you've learned.

Love Up

———————— *Read Deuteronomy 24:1–5* ————————

God laid down some specific rules about divorce in the first four verses of Deuteronomy 24. Why might they have come before the fifth verse: "When a man takes a bride, he must not go out with the army or be liable for any duty. He is free to stay at home for one year, so that he can bring joy to the wife he has married" (Deuteronomy 24:5 HCSB)?

....
....
....
....

Why do you think God established this quality time for newlyweds?

....
....
....
....

What does this tell you about God's view of your happiness?

....
....
....
....

Dancing Your Heart Out

———————— *Read 2 Samuel 6* ————————

When was the last time you danced with wild abandon? What prompted it?

....

....

....

What was the difference between David's and Michal's attitude and heart on this occasion?

....

....

When, if ever, have the opinions or attitudes of others inhibited your dancing?

....

....

What did David choose to do when Michal challenged his expression of joy? What will you do the next time someone challenges your choice?

....

....

....

Even Though

—————— *Read Habakkuk 3:1–19* ——————

What questions do you have for God in this moment? How do those questions differ from the ones that were on your mind yesterday?

....

....

....

....

What troubles are surrounding you today? In what ways might you cling to and focus on them?

....

....

....

....

What might you need to change in your life so that you can be like Habakkuk, rejoicing in God, rising up to the heights, free from discouragement and embracing joy?

....

....

....

....

Continual Joy

——— *Read 1 Thessalonians 5:16–18* ———

In 1 Thessalonians 5:16–18 (AMPC), Paul told believers to rejoice always, to "be unceasing in prayer," and to "thank [God] in everything [no matter what the circumstances may be." How might constant rejoicing, praying, and thanking—no matter what you're experiencing—work together to fill your life with joy?

....

....

....

....

....

....

....

Which of these three—rejoicing, praying, and thanking—are you doing well? Which need work?

....

....

....

....

....

....

Better Things Await

—————— *Read Hebrews 10:34* ——————

Think back to a time when you suffered terribly. What kept you faithful during those days? Who came along to stand with you? How, if ever, have you helped others going through the same thing?

....

....

....

....

....

....

How might knowing there are "better things waiting for you that will last forever" (Hebrews 10:34 NLT) help you hang on to joy no matter what happens?

....

....

....

....

....

....

....

For Endurance's Sake

———— *Read James 1:1–18* ————

James said there *is* "an opportunity for great joy" while you're enduring trials and tribulations (James 1:2 NLT). What makes that so?

....

....

....

....

How might this knowledge change your ideas about adversity? How might it make you stronger?

....

....

....

....

God promises blessings and a future reward for "those who patiently endure testing and temptation" (James 1:12 NLT). What might be your reward for endurance today?

....

....

....

....

Amid Suffering

—————— *Read 1 Peter 4* ——————

Why are you surprised when trials come your way?

....

....

....

....

In what ways have you armed yourself with the same attitude Christ had when He suffered physical pain? How does that attitude help you?

....

....

....

....

....

What is your reward for being a sufferer with Christ—now and later? If you are suffering, what does Peter tell you to do (1 Peter 4:19)?

....

....

....

....

Mind Transformation

Read Romans 12:1–2

Throughout the Bible, God tells you to rejoice, to be joyful. To get there from wherever you are each morning takes daily mind renewal. What do you do to turn your body and mind over to God?

....

....

....

....

....

....

....

In what ways do you find yourself conforming to the world? What might you want to pull away from so you can get closer to God?

....

....

....

....

....

....

....

Called to Rejoice

———————— *Read Romans 12:9–15* ————————

Paul listed several marks of a true Christian in Romans 12. Links to joy come up twice. The first is "rejoice in hope" (v. 12 ESV)—no matter what is happening in your life. How successful are you in this duty?

....

....

....

....

....

....

....

The second link calls believers to "rejoice with those who rejoice, weep with those who weep" (v. 15 ESV). What does this tell you about the value God puts on empathy and compassion?

....

....

....

....

....

....

Looking on the Bright Side

—————— *Read Philippians 1:12–18* ——————

Because Paul continued to preach about Jesus in prison, he spread the Good News *and* his boldness gave others courage to speak out. In this he rejoiced! When have you looked at a not-so-positive circumstance in your life and found the good?

....

....

....

....

....

....

....

If Paul hadn't been imprisoned, he might never have written believers encouraging letters. How does this realization change your perspective of Paul's suffering—and your own?

....

....

....

....

....

....

In God's House

———————— *Read Psalm 84* ————————

Why does your being with God give you more joy than anything else on earth?

....

....

....

....

In what ways is God your sun and shield?

....

....

....

....

Psalm 84:12 (AMPC) says that trust in God is "leaning and believing on [Him], committing all and confidently looking to [Him], and that without fear or misgiving." Which of these words or phrases speaks to your heart, helping you define what trust is in your own life?

....

....

....

....

By Choosing Thoughts

———————— *Read Philippians 4:4-9* ————————

Paul commanded believers to be full of joy—always! But that's difficult if you're fixing your thoughts on the wrong things. What type of things do you often find yourself dwelling on?

....

....

....

....

What might wrong thinking lead you to?

....

....

....

....

If your mind is too often fixed on the world's troubles, what can you do to change things around? How might doing so help not just you but also those you love?

....

....

....

....

By Choosing the Right Help

— *Read Psalm 20–21* —

In Psalm 20, King David's followers prayed for his success, that God would help him in battle and fulfill his heart's desire. Psalm 21 describes the results of the requests made in Psalm 20. When have you trusted in something or someone other than God? What were the results?

....
....
....
....

In what did David find joy (Psalm 21)?

....
....
....
....

How has God fulfilled your heart's desire when you trusted in Him alone?

....
....
....
....

Amid Contentment

———— *Read Ecclesiastes 5:18–20* ————

How content are you with your life? In what ways do you choose to find enjoyment in the blessings that God has allotted you?

....

....

....

....

When do you find joy in your work? To whom do you attribute your resources—earthly and heavenly?

....

....

....

....

In what ways does God keep you "occupied with the joy of [your] heart" (Ecclesiastes 5:20 HCSB)? How is "the tranquillity of God. . . mirrored in [you]" (Ecclesiastes 5:20 AMPC)?

....

....

....

....

Strengths and Patience

──────────── *Read Isaiah 30:18, 29* ────────────

Having chosen to trust God above anything and anyone else, turning to Him and resting in Him, you'll be saved by Him. What does God, through Isaiah, tell you will be your strengths—if you choose to choose them?

....

....

....

....

....

....

....

God is patiently waiting for you to come to Him so He can bless you and give you joy. How patiently do you wait for *Him*?

....

....

....

....

....

....

Along with the Right Diet

— *Read Jeremiah 15:16; Ezekiel 2:8; 3:1–3; Revelation 10:9* —

When does your spirit crave God's Word the most? In what ways and how often do you feed it God's Word?

....

....

....

....

....

What joy does your soul derive from scriptures? What verses speak to you the most? Why?

....

....

....

....

When have God's words given you a bit of indigestion? Why do you think they were hard to swallow?

....

....

....

....

When Considering Plans

———— *Read Jeremiah 29* ————

How comforting is it knowing God has plans for you, "plans for good and not for disaster, to give you a future and a hope" (Jeremiah 29:11 NLT)? How might choosing to focus on the joy of this promise keep you from worrying about the future?

....

....

....

....

....

In what ways does God communicate His plans for you to you?

....

....

....

....

Are you seeking God with all your heart? If so, how?

....

....

....

....

Trading In Your Mourning

—— *Read Jeremiah 31* ——

How does it feel knowing that God loves you "with an everlasting love" and continues His "faithfulness to you" (Jeremiah 31:3 ESV)?

....

....

....

....

....

In what ways does God "rebuild you" so that you can dance and be happy once more (Jeremiah 31:4 NLT)? How happy does it make you knowing God *wants* you to be happy?

....

....

....

....

When has God found a way to turn your mourning into joy?

....

....

....

....

Instead of Disbelief—Part 1

—————————— *Read Acts 12* ——————————

·What have you been in earnest prayer about? How did those petitions before God affect the situation? How did they affect you?

....

....

....

....

....

Imagine an angel coming to a troubled friend's rescue—because of your prayers! In what ways would that stir or increase your faith?

....

....

....

....

In what ways does being a part of, witnessing, or reading about a miracle affect your spiritual life?

....

....

....

....

Instead of Disbelief—Part 2

———— *Read Acts 12* ————

How might an amazing answer to prayer affect your future expectations?

....

....

....

....

When has your joy so disconcerted you that you went a little loco? How did others react to your behavior?

....

....

....

....

In what ways have others tried to convince you that the miracle you think you saw or experienced was in your imagination? How did it affect your joy?

....

....

....

....

Joy in the Midst of Sorrow

—————————— *Read 2 Samuel 19* ——————————

After successfully regaining his kingdom, King David was found weeping, mourning the death of his treasonous son Absalom. When have you experienced a loss of one thing and a victory of another—at the same time?

....

....

....

....

How did you respond—displaying grief for your loss or joy for your gain? How did your response affect others?

....

....

....

....

Both joy and sorrow can be contagious. Which would God have you express? Which do you naturally lean toward?

....

....

....

....

Above Finances

———— *Read 1 Timothy 6:3–21* ————

How might your concern over finances keep you from joyful contentment? In what ways is "godliness with contentment. . .a great gain" (1 Timothy 6:6 HCSB)?

....

....

....

....

When have you experienced or witnessed the spiritual law that the *love* of money is the root of all evil?

....

....

....

....

In what ways can you set your hope on God the Provider and not on "the uncertainty of wealth" (1 Timothy 6:17 HCSB)?

....

....

....

....

By Rising Up

—— *Read Isaiah 60* ——

Speaking through Isaiah, God said to "arise [from the depression and prostration in which circumstances have kept you—rise to a new life]! Shine. . .for your light has come" (Isaiah 60:1 AMPC). In what ways does God help you rise up out of your situations and into His light?

....

....

....

....

....

....

....

How does lifting your eyes—a change in focus, from your circumstances to God—lead you to capture God's joy?

....

....

....

....

....

....

Over Bitterness

—————— *Read Ruth 1* ——————

In Moab, Naomi lost her two sons and one husband. When she and daughter-in-law Ruth returned to Israel, she told her friends there, "Call me not Naomi [pleasant]; call me Mara [bitter], for the Almighty has dealt very bitterly with me" (Ruth 1:20 AMPC). When have you chosen bitterness instead of focusing on blessings?

....
....
....
....
....
....
....

How might listing all you have to be thankful for turn your bitterness into joy?

....
....
....
....
....
....

In God's Promises

———— *Read 2 Peter 1:3–5; Genesis 21:1–7* ————

When have you been so blessed by God that you began laughing? In what ways was that blessing an answer to prayer? How much of it had once seemed an impossibility?

....

....

....

....

In what ways have your blessings been a fulfillment of one or more of God's promises? What one promise in particular do you lean on? Why?

....

....

....

....

How does standing on God's promises keep you in His joy?

....

....

....

....

Within New Realities

—— *Read Psalm 126* ——

In what ways do you believe God has restored your fortunes? How might His doing so have made you so full of laughter and joy that you felt you were living in a dream? In what ways did that dream *become* your new reality?

....

....

....

....

....

....

....

God knows life can be very hard. Yet how glad are you knowing that if you plant while weeping, you'll reap a harvest of joy?

....

....

....

....

....

....

Over Discouragement—Part 1

—————— *Read Psalm 42* ——————

The writer of Psalm 42 questioned why he was so discouraged. Then he revealed how his enemies were continually teasing him, asking, "Where is this God of yours?" (Psalm 42:3 NLT). When have others asked you that question? What was your response, if any?

....

....

....

....

....

....

....

To pull himself out of discouragement, the psalmist began questioning the sad state of his heart, his inner self. When have you found yourself doing the same?

....

....

....

....

....

....

Over Discouragement—Part 2

—————————— *Read Psalm 42* ——————————

Consider making a list of things that are discouraging you. Then make a list of things that encourage you. How might doing so help you turn back to putting your focus on hope instead of despair?

....

....

....

....

How does it feel knowing that each day God pours out His forever love on you?

....

....

....

....

How would putting your hope in God, affirming that you will praise Him again soon, help you recover your joy?

....

....

....

....

And Contentment

———— *Read Philippians 4:10–20* ————

When has the concern of others for you given you joy? When those people helped you—by praying for you, providing for you, loving you, etc.—how did you respond to their care?

....

....

....

....

....

How content are you in this life? Have you learned how to be not just satisfied but happy with little or lots?

....

....

....

....

Who or what gives you the strength to do what you're called to do?

....

....

....

....

With a Happy Tune

—————————— *Read James 5:7-20* ——————————

Where does prayer come on your to-do list when you're in trouble? Who supports you, prays over you, and anoints you when you're sick?

....
....
....
....

What do you do naturally when you're happy? Have you ever sung praises to God?

....
....
....
....

List all the things that bring you joy. From that list, compose a song of praise. Then sing it, reflecting your joy to God, the Master of love.

....
....
....
....